ALSO BY SUSAN MILLAR DuMARS

POETRY

Big Pink Umbrella (Salmon, 2008)

Dreams for Breakfast (Salmon, 2010)

The God Thing (Salmon, 2013)

SHORT STORIES

Lights in the Distance (Doire Press, 2010)

AS EDITOR

*Over the Edge - The First Ten Years
– An anthology of fiction & poetry*
(Salmon, 2013)

salmonpoetry

*Celebrating 35 Years
of Literary Publishing*

Bone Fire

Susan Millar DuMars

Published in 2016 by
Salmon Poetry
Cliffs of Moher, County Clare, Ireland
Website: www.salmonpoetry.com
Email: info@salmonpoetry.com

ISBN 978-1-910669-41-9

COVER ARTWORK: © *Mario Lopes | Dreamstime.com*
COVER DESIGN & TYPESETTING: *Siobhán Hutson*
Printed in Ireland by Sprint Print

Salmon Poetry gratefully acknowledges the support of
The Arts Council / An Chomhairle Ealaoín

Again, for Kevin
my present
and future

Acknowledgements

Thanks are due to the editors of the following publications, in which some of these poems have previously appeared:
Bogman's Cannon, Cafe Review (US), *Crannóg, Headstuff, Skylight 47, St. Sebastian's Review* (US).

"Migration" was written for, and will appear in, *Thinking Continental: Essays and Poems*, an anthology to be published in 2017 by the University of Nebraska.

"Reasons To Tend The Front Garden" was a finalist for a WOW award in 2014.

"Reverse" was commissioned by Democrats Abroad as part of a commemoration of the fiftieth anniversary of the death of John F. Kennedy; it was first published on their website.

My personal thanks to Drucilla Wall, Hannah Kiely, Robyn Rowland; Siobhán Hutson and Jessie Lendennie of Salmon Poetry. I'm so grateful to all of the Skylight Poets, past and present, for their editing help and their support.

Finally, my profound thanks to my late friend, poet Kevin O'Shea, who worked on many of these poems too.

Contents

Orchard 10

Questionnaire 11

In His Attic 12

Reverse 13

Thirst 14

Bobby Sands in South Philadelphia 16

His Blackbirds 18

Bone Fire 19

Pigeons 20

Patterns 21

Baby Makes Me Watch 22

I Thought This Was Love 23

Under the Awning 24

Stripes and Stars 25

The Rejection 26

Mule Deer 28

A Lot 29

Barefoot 30

Don't Tell the Witch 31

let the dog 32

The First Rule 33

Lemons 34

Bathing   35

Reclamation   36

Forty-Niner   37

Instant   38

Meet You   39

Retreat   42

Migration   43

Night Woods   45

Stars In Your Bucket   46

Tender   48

Reasons to Tend the Front Garden   49

Even In June   50

October Third   51

Twins   52

Moon, Alone   54

My Voice That's No Longer a Ribbon   55

Pandora Packs It In   56

Until Then   57

Don't Try to be Good   58

Orchard

I torched our orchard last night.
The first flames were feathers
fallen from some bright,
fabled bird.
The trees wept sparks and apples
and I said goodbye
to the faces in the bark.

Soon it was a field of light
like the glass sunsets of winter
when you'd be tucked in safe
while I wandered the orchard,
protecting our perimeter.

The fire panted, a great animal
and I thought of the time,
my head in your lap,
a kind-eyed lion
was painted on the sky.
I thought it was sent to keep us safe,
believed in guardians then,
spells, the voices
of branches. And you.
None of that matters now.

Last night I torched the orchard.
It's gone now. I'm not sure
it was ever there.

Questionnaire

You appear to be screaming.
Are you screaming?
Why are you screaming?

Is that blood?
Really,
that seems an extreme
response.

On a scale of one to –
please stop screaming.
How can you answer
if you can't hear my questions?
I'm really quite interested
in your point of view.

Have you fallen?
You know, that floor
is quite sticky.
You don't seem
to be taking this
seriously.

Why are you screaming?
There's no space
on my form
for that.

On a scale of one to ten,
ten being highest,
how much did we
hurt you?

You appear to be crying.
Why are you crying?
Will you
stop soon?

In His Attic

He holds the parcel out to me
and it is my heart,
swaddled in blue tissue.
Cold, white,
quietly convulsing.

Look! Been saving
this, all these years.
Not a scratch on it.

Boxes and boxes
behind him — full
of us. Captured.

I've been so careful.
He smiles at the fist
of twitching muscle
in my hands.

It is, indeed,
unbroken.

Reverse

The black car rolls back.
Pieces of scalp
reassemble.
Leaden splinters slide free,
sing in blue air,
find home
with a cheerful pop.
Children unplug their ears.
Tears retreat up faces.
Blood wings away
from the woman's stockings,
her small, neat gloves.
The man beside her sits up,
waves at crowds suddenly happy.

The woman looks ahead,
sees nothing
but endless white Texan sun.

Thirst

Dusty Millar's head on fire.
His eyes two wet worlds,
beckoning.

He sits by the bar.
In his battering hands
the immaculate pint.

The bomb's just gone off.
Its pulse sharpening
the air like a stone
sharpens a knife.
It also shattered
the front window,
pulled free a ceiling beam,
brought down the back room
where it was hidden.
There's a lot of light.
Sudden light.
In what was
a dark corner pub.

Dusty sips his pint.
It's that moment
of stillness before
screams and sirens
and the flailing arms
of the near dead
as they try to swim
through smoke
to the safe
Mackey Street shore.

It's peaceful,
and Dusty's the only
thing moving.
He makes a little whisper-sigh
after he swallows.

His hair is red as brick,
as flame,
and his eyes are my eyes.
He smiles at me
and I feel the cold caress,
in my two hands, of a glass.

This story probably isn't true.
But it's all I have of you,
Granddad, so I retell it.

This tale passed down
of you shrugging off
a Belfast bomb
is all I've inherited —

that, and this thirst.

Bobby Sands in South Philadelphia

Betty'd come over
on the boat, like Mom.
Why should I feel sorry
for him? A criminal.
He killed people.
Why should I
feel sorry?
She had opinions.
Mom had none.

Not when the vacant
warehouse burned.
Smoke glittered
in our living room.
I wanted to stay,
to lie on my back and watch it
satiate the open space
but was yanked like a tooth
from our house, sent to sleep
on a neighbour's floor
wrapped in borrowed blanket
siren lights reflecting
and no one knew
how that fire got started.
No one saw a thing.

My mom smuggled cupcakes
home in her handbag
when they had a birthday
party at work. We ate
them greedily, licking bright
icing off swaddling napkins.

I couldn't imagine
being hungry on purpose.

His Blackbirds

after Wallace Stevens

He rides with the top down;
the car fills up with blackbirds.

The truth is a hard beak.

My skin smarts from too much sun.
The truth is a peripheral
wing-flap.

He and I are one.
He and I and his blackbirds are one.

And I close my eyes, try to hover
above his voice, that moving thing –
but I can't fly higher
than the blackbird.

His history unfolds its dark feathers.
He drives on uphill, alone.

He and I are two. But I'm bound
by the blackbird's whistle.

I don't know which to prefer;
the beauty of beauty or the beauty of fact.
The lying sun or the honest blackbirds.

Bone Fire

Sky closes in
like a drawstring bag.
Now I've sucked the meat
off each bone,
I burn the year's skeleton.

Smoke that winds
around my wrist
becomes your hand.

And you won't let go.

Pigeons

The dead are crows that gather, mutter, steal
scatter when you try to ask
them anything. It hurts to hear their peals —
nails dragged up the sky's blue glass.

Worse than the dead are the dead-to-you.
However long you've been apart
allow these pigeons to circle and coo
and they'll scavenge your softest parts.

Patterns

The room of us is empty
but I sit on the rug sometimes
feel the sun through blindless
windows heat my skin,
make patterns on me.

The room of us is empty
but, admit it, you still visit —
stretch out flat in all that space
let the wooden floor support you
breathe along with you.

Something of us
lives on in there.
The room is empty
but not bare.

Baby Makes Me Watch

His features a pattern of cracks in a mirror.
My eyes give up my own reflection
to trace, retrace the hairline breaks.

I'm on my back and the door is a cloud.
I try but I can't reach it.

Baby says I'm his shining comet
and I have all his faith.
Baby says I force him
to tell secrets he'd rather forget.
Baby makes me watch.
The door's a cloud – I'm cold.
Baby makes sure I know
this is all my fault.

Baby, you have to let me go.

Baby makes me watch.

I Thought This Was Love

He said my elbows
bruised him —
hated my bones, wished
I'd lose them

so he could wear me
like a scarf —
good news was,
he loved my laugh

loved my voice, when I
whispered stories
as his hive-head
buzzed worry —

it helped him sleep.
His eyelids fluttered.
Awake, I watched them.

His dreams mattered.

Under the Awning

His skin yellow like worn piano keys;
her hair long and black. They drink gold beer
from small glasses. He smokes. Cold ash
on the table, wet circles. Their heads
together like children telling secrets.
They speak in murmurs softer than the rain.

His voice and the storm, the memory of these,
will stay on her shoulders
like her hair – heavy.
Shining.

Stripes and Stars

Trumpet, blood, the reveille
for American boys in basement rooms –
stars behind their skin, their eyes.
At night the flag sings lullabies
to the near-men in their dream cocoons –
songs of Iwo Jima,
hymns about the moon.

Wake up! You boys in basement rooms.
Climb the umbilical steps to breakfast.
Stripes of bacon on a white plate.
By day
hand on heart like a swung-shut gate
you pledge your allegiance
like son, like father
like swing batter batter
like air guitar hero
like kung fu fighter

like who am I who am I
student loaned soldier
like *for God sake keep it together*
tell no one tell no one
the flagpole at night clanks *lonely, lonely*
and you shove your dresser against the door.

My American boys, behind your skin
flicker warmer lights than stars.

The Rejection

for C.

My hand —
that small animal —
scuttled across your back
clutched your shoulder
like it was a rock
on the shore
and the tide
racing in.

My mouth —
that soft messenger —
kissed the plane of your face
the crease by your eye.

I wanted you
like a safety pin
to pierce
and tether me
to the dry cloth
of solid life.

You shook your head
took my hand –
that small, trembling animal –
soothed each finger still
pressed the palm-heart
against your palm-heart
and held.

You and I
don't do that
you said, your eyes
on mine.

I watched your lips move
my white depths escaping
in a single tear.
How I wanted you
to save me.

How splendidly
you did.

Mule Deer

for Rob

Imagine, baby brother, that your mind
is not a barren place but woods where warm
eyes watch you; where mule deer gallop past you,
their softness brushing softness you forgot
to hide. Where ice is licked to quench their thirst.
Their hungry mouths taste green beneath the snow.

Imagine them at home in that sparse winter
you keep inside; that place so starved of light.

They run for pleasure, their blood hammering,
sure hooves sparking hard ground.

A Lot

I don't tell him I never liked her,
that his flat reeks of cat
piss; that he looks tired.
I hug him fast but don't
hold his hand when he tells me
about the divorce, the friends
he lost in the settlement,
the kids (adjusting), the job (a grind).
I don't tell him how much
his new girl reminds me
of his ex.

I don't say that I've been sad
too – I have, though my life
is Facebook friendly.
A lot has happened,
to me too.

I don't tell him that.

Barefoot

Here she comes.
Joy, tripping down the field to me.
Her face light and bone.
She smells of rain
and oranges
her voice hard
and warm
like a wooden chair left out
in the sun.

Here she is.
Joy touches me
with her tiny starfish hands
and she is barefoot grass
first bite chocolate
every song I loved when I was ninteteen.

She holds me
and I am peeking through a keyhole
at eternity's shine.

Don't Tell the Witch

after Anne Sexton

Don't tell the witch, but we're alright.
The cat, he chases milk bottle tops;
the sly, fat mice thrive out of sight.
Gangly grass and dandelion clocks
waggle and giggle, front and rear.
Don't tell the witch — we're flourishing here

in our big cracked house, red onion skins
autumn-crackle under stockinged feet.
Teabags plop like rotten teeth from the bin's
laughing mouth. By husband's seat —

heels of brown bread toasted black,
stanzas scribbled on the phone bill's back,
apple skewered on a kitchen knife.
No spell stronger than this loved life.

let the dog

he gets me to take off
my panties by saying
c'mon — let the dog
see the rabbit
skin to skin
bellies bucking

we laugh so hard
it's like coming

and sex is no
cuddle

sex is no
planting of seeds

sex is not porn —

girl cock-endoscopied
her eyes so bored

sex does not
keep a straight face

we laugh so hard
breathless sprawled
and now my rabbit
wants his dog

The First Rule

Will I show you what to do
with a naked woman?

You can
lie on top of her
feel her yield
taste her salt
ride her undulations
know her to be ocean
almost drown

leave her
the wind again her breath
the tide again her muscles
the rocks again her bones.

This is a naked woman.
Rain fed
pulsing soft.

Respect, sailor,
is the first rule of the sea.

Lemons

Morning sun licks gold
the lemons in the white bowl.

Slice one; it holds
its wet segments tight.

Clock face promising
there's still time.

Bathing

Bare ass on the cold edge
of the tub; air
up my spine
my leg turns raw red
in the water
breasts dangle heavy
I'm gripping the sides –

finding I'm holding onto things more,
the animation of my life
gone herky-jerky, each frame stuttering.

Tiring
to carry yourself like a dozen eggs.

I swing my other leg in
and the water scalds the skin.

For a moment I'm a goddess
rising from a lake of fire.

Reclamation

The blood has stopped
and with it the need
to suckle lesser creatures.
My breasts are pale, cool
proud
and mine.

The blood has stopped
and with it the need
to shield smaller souls
inside me.
My womb calm.
Not weeping.
And it's my womb.

I'm learning the pleasure
of empty.
The weight of one.
Nothing on my back
but a breeze
getting colder.

The blood has stopped
and with it the need
to grow anything
but older.

Forty-Niner

I'm seven times
the seven year old
who courted mud
talked to God
felt the hump of Earth
against her back
lifted yellow leaves
from mucky puddles
as if, among reflected clouds
she'd found gold.

Welcome back, prospector.
Forty-nine's a fine time
to ride out of the city
get dirty
pan some solitary creek
for lustre.

instant

when the wind slows
these mad cracks in the sky
these nicks of pure light
become snowflakes
one and two and three
drifting

when the wind slows
all these mad cracks in my sky
become moments
one and two and three
and I am drifting
into each

bright soft melting
that has led me here

watching that red taxi
its lights on
edging down the hill

Meet You

I'll meet you under the disused
railway bridge; remember
we knitted fingers there
and talked harmonic convergence?
The planets were aligning
for us
you said
and I wanted –
The stones were dark and damp.

Okay then
how about at Friendly's?
Where I ordered chocolate
got vanilla
but the waitress looked like
she'd had a bad day?
Oh my god, you said
if you can't
send back a milkshake –

I'll meet you halfway.
You know that place
the health food store that smells
like oily coffee and the little booth
where I bought the yin-yang earrings?
You wore one and I wore one.
God, no.
What about you?
Is yours gone too?

Okay
I'll come up the hill
and meet you in Bonducci's
where you once challenged me
to write a vampire poem
and I did, on the spot.
You liked it, I recall.
All blood and longing.
I said I hadn't found
my subject matter yet.
Could be a great writer
when I'm old,
like, over forty.
You shook your head
said life is happening now.

Well, how about outside
the hot tub place?
It was snowing
we smuggled in wine,
some Peter Gabriel –
stayed at opposite ends
though afterward admitted
we both wanted –
wanted –
don't know why we didn't.
But the walk home.
All that snow.

I'll tell you, let's meet
at the lesbian boarding house.
Remember for a laugh
you left the seat up?
Your smile split the air
and oh my god
I wanted to tell you –
I wanted to say –

No, no problem
I can come to you.
Listen
I'm on my way

just stay there.

Retreat

I don't know the names of things here. Language fails. Don't know the name of this cove, that mountain nor his brothers, those flowers – tiny blood red bells. The hidden birds that click, click. That island of yellow stone in the midst of blue water. I know water. Wind, grass, field. I know sky.

Don't know the name of this feeling. The hard nut cracking open inside me. The sudden liquid of experience, without and within. The need to hold it close, the need to give it away. This cracking open.

I don't know how to get home from here. I expect that when I do get home, home will have changed too. And I won't know the words.

I know the moon last night was bright enough to wake me. Padded outside in borrowed slippers. Heard the water lapping and the thump of the pier against the shore. I know the moon was telling me the clouds had broken. Proud little silver sky-comma. Showing off her scatter of full stop stars. Words. There were no words then, at four in the morning. The water was a mirror and I suddenly happy.

I know that Connemara is softer than I remembered. Or maybe it's me.

Maybe softness recognizes softness. Without words.

Migration

i. Grand Canyon (United States)

On the South Rim,
snow falls fast
and the ruts in the path
hammocked by ice make me clutch
at the offered arms
of oaks. No guard rail
between me and consequence.

Nothing hidden –
I'm face to face
with time's hard carving.
Just me and the scream
of the red tailed hawk.
Now, the naked canyon
slips from cloud-shadow
bed clothes –
reveals
her iron blush.

ii. Barna Woods (Europe)

The trees — wet brush strokes
on white sky — taper, drip dark.
Green moss, sudden and sweet
as a lover's tongue.
Beech limbs steal
light from ash.
Sparrow hawks joke
in their own language.

Every side of every war
has buried the inconvenient
here. I tread on bones,
hidden histories.

On the slush of secrets
and sodden leaves.

Night Woods

after Ted Hughes

My path was direct
through the bones of the murdered,
the maimed; I nest among remains.

Meditation, prayer are no use here.
All my questions go unanswered
except by the blip of blood-fear, the scream

of collared kill, carried above trees
by the hawk. And it laughs as it dives,
laughs, for the pleasure of swooping,

the pleasure of choosing,
the heat that escapes as it pierces the creature.
For the meat. This is its nature.

I, the hawk's witness. This is my nature.

Stars In Your Bucket

littered
among the grass
bent stars
to be collected
in your bucket
where they fatten
in the water
start to breathe
start to shudder
broken stars
in your bucket

shine them up
little yellow
stars like badges
TV sheriffs
fix
near their hearts
don't use polish
just the water
make them glisten
baby stars
make them bright

spread them out
on the counter
promise them
heavens
a ladder
glue to stick them
promise

little broken stars
safest in the bucket
under your bed
sing to them
sad songs

one day
promise them
they will diamond
the sky

Tender

Cry for the way it curls,
cradles the air.
For the skin – thirsty, veined,
puckered in places.
For the radiating ribs
(the galaxy they enclose),
for the spine
still strong
enough to hold,
remember.

Grieve for the forming,
greening,
falling,
dying.
Most clearly itself
in the moment the muck
swallows it back.

Cry for a late leaf
tangled in wet grass
in a field outside Seattle.
Kneel and kiss
its tender edge.

Reasons to Tend the Front Garden

Because it's here. Because I'm here.
Because it's my house now.
Because yellow petals shimmer,
like fish scales,
after rain.

Dried twig crackle, riddle
of weeds, shrubs skeletal
after a tough winter.
Because the dead must make room
for the living.
Because roots need room to take hold.
Because I'm moved by the humility
of a trimmed lawn.
Because I love
sun and the shadows of clouds
moving, everything moving,

growing, changing, dying,
and I am part of everything.
Because I love
the sweet mourning
in the scent of cut grass.
Because I love.
Because I'm here.

Even In June

she mentions autumn
and I see the sky's hard glaze
feel the forked wind
sense the hurrying twilight
and before long
I'll be ordering a turkey
a tin of foil wrapped chocolates
I'm not ready
too fast
this turning
this knowing you're not
moving forward
but around

can we just rest here
though even in June
petals drop
the seagull casts a shadow
it will end
and then
when you're
just that bit more tired

it will start again

October Third

for Kevin

face of old paper
boiled eyes
watching things
I can't see
mouth slack
arms open across
the backs of the molded
plastic chairs
he dozes
comments on the rugby
dozes

I'm fine
until I have to leave without him
surrender him to a process
of liquids measured
going in
coming out
things under the tongue
under the skin
hall with a halo
of heat, piss, sick

his foot pokes
over the end
of the trolley
his ankle white as a turnip
pried from nurturing dirt

I'm fine
till I get to the carpark

Twins

i

The Sun falls stillborn from my belly —
cools. The ball of him dims.

Moon, his twin
sucks her fingers —
we hear the throb of distant tides.

ii

He was all I am, and better —
glimpsed, then gone.

Leave me alone.

Your well-meaning eyes
reminders — a sky
of small suns.

iii

Moon is unexpected.
Her water-white light
strange, exquisite
even when no one
is looking —

present.

iv

How to be her mum, and his —

to mourn what's lost,
love what is?

Moon, Alone

Although she drags the heaving sea behind her
she feels reduced, a lozenge on the tongue
of God; a sugar circle melting bright.
A light dissolving – kind, and turning kinder

for kind is all she ever wished to be.
Not wild, bewitching, not an opal shine
alone and distant. Creatures howl with need
beneath what seems a milk-soft mystery.

But Sister Moon is no mystery.
She's just a girl alone in the dark.
The night has teeth. It bites and bites till Moon's
reduced – a smile without eyes to see.

She had a brother once – quite blonde, quite bright.
The sun fell down, so now there's only night.

My Voice That's No Longer A Ribbon

Who sings you to sleep now?
Slides her voice
like a ribbon
beneath your bolted door?

Just a ribbon
frivolous
but soft, cool
threaded white through your fingers.

My voice is lightning now
still bright
woven through the fingers
of the sky.
Coupled with thunder's throat clearings

my words tremble electric
show you in a flash
the truth of your prison.

Sweetheart,
who sings to you now in your cell?
I wish you had climbed down my voice
when it was ribbon.
Wish I could've freed you, somehow.

Pandora Packs It In

This chaos
is not my chaos.
This cyclone of bats
their flap-flap
their help-me expressions
and squeaks.
This blackened sky
cold shade
palsies, plagues —
nothing to do with me.

I'm not made from clay
but bile and blood.
I suffer. I seethe.
I can leave.
Chuck the box. Tell sulking gods
I'm not playing.

The last thing released
was a bird.
Not the bluebird of happiness.
A magpie. Yes.
She and I
will make our own luck.
She'll show me how to gather
things that shine
reflect me back at me.

Until Then

for Kevin

It will end, as all things do,
in the sunset robes of death.

It will end with a solitary tree
on a hilltop.

It will end like a game of soldiers,
the little men and their machines
deprived of the breath of a child's belief.

It will end as a dance ends
as partners bow
and start to remember
where their separate bodies
begin
and end.

Until then, hold me.

Don't Try To Be Good

i.

Why do you bruise
your feet on sharp stones
when the sand is warm,
forgiving?
It's the same length
either way.

The sun is low.
Your silhouette slow-dances
across the beach.

Don't try to be good.
You already are.
Even your shadow's
full of grace.

ii.

Don't ask, *why is this happening to me?*
It's natural you should wonder
but the only real answer

is misfortune cures you
like smoke
makes that meaty heart of yours
taste saltier
keep longer.

That is all.
And does it matter why?
What matters
is what you do next.

SUSAN MILLAR DuMARS has published three previous collections with Salmon Poetry, the most recent of which, *The God Thing*, appeared in March, 2013. She published a book of short stories, *Lights in the Distance*, with Doire Press in 2010, and was a featured fiction writer on *Atticus Review* in late 2014. She is currently at work on a second story collection. Her work has been widely anthologized. Born in Philadelphia, Susan lives in Galway, Ireland, where she and her husband Kevin Higgins have coordinated the Over the Edge readings series since 2003. She is the editor of the 2013 anthology *Over the Edge: The First Ten Years*, published by Salmon.